52 Hands-On

Bulletin Board Designs

BY LISA HAHN

Illustrated by Karen Pauls

CONCORDIA PUBLISHING HOUSE · SAINT LOUIS

Copyright © 1994 Concordia Publishing House
3558 S. Jefferson Avenue, St. Louis, MO 63118-3968
Manufactured in the United States of America

3   4   5   6   7   8   9   10   11   12   12   11   10   09   08   07   06   05   04   03

Contents

A NOTE TO TEACHERS

Don't just stand there! I have often stood in front of a bulletin board or a seasonally decorated corner of a classroom and heard these words shouting inside my head. This collection of bulletin board ideas will not only keep your students busy during those "extra 10 minutes," but will also keep them exploring and learning.

Some of these bulletin boards will encourage your class to work together to reach a goal. Others will be made largely by the students themselves. Some boards will help the children celebrate the faith and new life God has given them through His Son. Others will help them learn about the world God created for them.

God has led me to share these ideas. I hope you and your students find them useful and enjoyable.

— Lisa Hahn

Encouragement Tree

OBJECTIVE

Children will write positive comments on leaves to encourage classmates in sharing God's love.

DIRECTIONS

1. Arrange words from 2 Thess. 1:3b on bulletin board.
2. Staple a large construction-paper tree trunk to bulletin board.
3. Place a basket of paper scraps in fall colors near the bulletin board.
4. Explain to your children that they will tear out leaf shapes, write encouraging messages to classmates on them, and staple them to the tree.

Your faith is growing more and more, and the love every one of you has for each other is increasing.

So I Say to You: Live by the Spirit

OBJECTIVE

Children will finger-paint pumpkins, giving them faces that express the fruit of the Spirit described in Gal. 5:22–23: love, joy, peace, patience, kindness, goodness, faithfulness, gentleness, self-control.

DIRECTIONS

1. Arrange title on bulletin board.
2. Staple construction-paper grass to board.
3. Staple a vine made from green yarn and construction-paper leaves across board.
4. Help children finger-paint individual pumpkins.
5. When pumpkins are dry, children use markers, crayons, or construction paper scraps to create features expressing a fruit of the Spirit.
6. Help each child write one fruit of the Spirit on a large construction paper leaf and attach leaf and pumpkin to vine.

What Does It Mean?

OBJECTIVE

Children will assemble parts of Martin Luther's coat of arms and explain the meaning of each part. Gold circle: Gold is precious. A circle is an endless shape. The golden circle reminds us of heaven's endless joy. Blue circle: The color blue reminds us that we will live with Jesus in heaven one day. White rose: The rose of Sharon reminds us that faith in Jesus brings joy, comfort, and peace. Red heart: We live because Jesus shed His blood for us. Our faith in Him saves us. Black cross: We are saved because Jesus died on the cross to pay the price for our sin.

DIRECTIONS

1. Place title on board.
2. Make a large model of Luther's coat of arms. Cut enlarged patterns from the next page from construction paper: Gold circle, blue circle, white rose, red heart, black cross. Explain the meaning of one part each day and add it to the board.
3. Let younger children trace the individual parts and add them to the board. Divide older children into 5 groups, assigning each group 1 shape from the coat of arms. Ask children to trace their group's shape and write on it something they have learned about their own faith—Jesus died for me. I will live in heaven forever, etc.
4. Ask children to attach their shapes around the large model on the board.

Patterns for Luther's Coat of Arms

Faith: What Does It Mean?

OBJECTIVE

Children will create their own coats of arms to express their faith in Jesus.

DIRECTIONS

1. Place title and a copy of Martin Luther's coat of arms on bulletin board.
2. Ask children to use 3 or 4 colors of construction paper and 3 or 4 shapes to design a coat of arms that expresses their own faith. (You might suggest that the children use red if they wish to symbolize sin. The use of black can be offensive.)
3. Help each child add a key that explains the meaning of their colors and shapes. Display coats of arms and keys on bulletin board.

Today Let's Thank Him for . . .

OBJECTIVE

Children will make a November calendar that displays things for which they are thankful.

DIRECTIONS

1. Number pieces of fall-colored construction paper from 1 to 30. Arrange under title on bulletin board to form a calendar for the month of November.
2. Ask children to draw pictures a bit smaller than the calendar spaces, showing things for which they are thankful.
3. Collect pictures and ask children to add one picture a day.
4. As each picture is added, ask a child to say a prayer thanking God for that blessing.

Today Let's Thank Him for . . .

Sun.	Mon.	Tues.	Wed.	Thurs.	Fri.	Sat.
1	2	3	4	5	6	7
8	9	10	11	12	13	14
15	16	17	18	19	20	21
22	23	24	25	26	27	28
29	30					

I Thank God for You because . . .

OBJECTIVE

Children will share why they thank God for one another.

DIRECTIONS

1. Place title, a cornucopia, and fruit cut from construction paper on bulletin board.
2. Write each child's name on a large envelope. Ask children to decorate their envelopes. Staple the backs of the envelopes to the board.
3. Place small squares of paper in an extra envelope stapled to the board. Ask children to use the squares of paper to finish the sentence "I thank God for you because . . ." and place them in one another's envelopes.
4. Children may take their envelopes home before Thanksgiving.

I'm Thankful for . . .

OBJECTIVE

Children will write down things for which they thank God and attach them to board.

DIRECTIONS

1. Place title and a large construction-paper basket on board.
2. Cut a variety of vegetable shapes from construction paper.
3. From time to time give children a vegetable. Ask them to write a blessing for which they are thankful and staple vegetable at the top of the basket.

Count Our Feathers!

OBJECTIVE

Children will hang appropriate addends on board to reach a given sum.

DIRECTIONS

1. Place title on board.
2. Stick from 5–10 push pins on board. (The pins will serve as "pegs" from which children can hang turkeys.) Attach another pin at the right of the board on which to hang a sum.
3. Number construction paper squares from 1 to 20. Punch a hole at the top of each square. Place numbers in an envelope or small box next to the board.
4. Ask each child to cut out a turkey body and glue on from 1 to 7 feathers. Punch holes in the turkeys and store them in an envelope or box next to the board.
5. To play the game, one child hangs a sum on the board. Another child hangs up turkeys with appropriate numbers of feathers until the sum is reached.

Will You Help Us Home for Dinner?

OBJECTIVE

Children will respond to God's love in Jesus and work together to achieve a goal.

DIRECTIONS

1. Cut letters for bulletin board title from construction paper and place on board. Add cabin, path, and trees.
2. Copy the patterns for the pilgrim couple on page 16. Color and cut them out and pin to board at the beginning of the path.
3. Explain to children that one way we can say thank You to God for the great gift He gave us in sending Jesus to live, die, and rise again for us is to share His love with one another. Set a special behavior goal for the class each day. Perhaps children will listen well, share with one another, keep classroom centers neat, etc. Each time you observe the children living out God's love, ask a child to move the pilgrim couple a little closer to the cabin.
4. When the pilgrim couple reaches the cabin, have a special celebration and thank God for helping you grow in His love.

Will You Help Us Home for Dinner?

Patterns for Pilgrim Couple

Help Tom Get Dressed for Thanksgiving

OBJECTIVE

Children will respond to God's love and work together to achieve a goal.

DIRECTIONS

1. Place title on board. Make a construction-paper turkey and attach to board. Make 15–20 construction-paper feathers and keep in an envelope or box near board.

2. Explain to children that when we think of all the wonderful blessings God gives us and how much He loves us, His Holy Spirit helps us share that love with one another. Set a special goal for each day—welcome classroom visitors politely, keep desks clean, etc. Each time you observe the class meeting a goal, ask a child to add a feather to "Tom."

3. Plan a special Thanksgiving celebration when Tom is completely "dressed."

Artist of the Month

OBJECTIVE

Children will take turns creating their own bulletin boards.

DIRECTIONS

1. Place the heading "Artist of the Month" with room for child's name and current month on a small bulletin board or on a small section of a larger board. For a large class, designate an "Artist of the Week."
2. Let children take turns decorating their own bulletin board.

Can You Put Us in Order?

OBJECTIVE

Children will alphabetize spelling/vocabulary words.

DIRECTIONS

1. Place title and numbered circles on bulletin board.
2. Ask students to write new spelling or vocabulary words on cards. Pin the cards in random order at the bottom of the board.
3. Children may alphabetize words by pinning them to the numbered circles in correct order.
4. You may wish to adapt the game to place words from Bible memory verses in correct order.

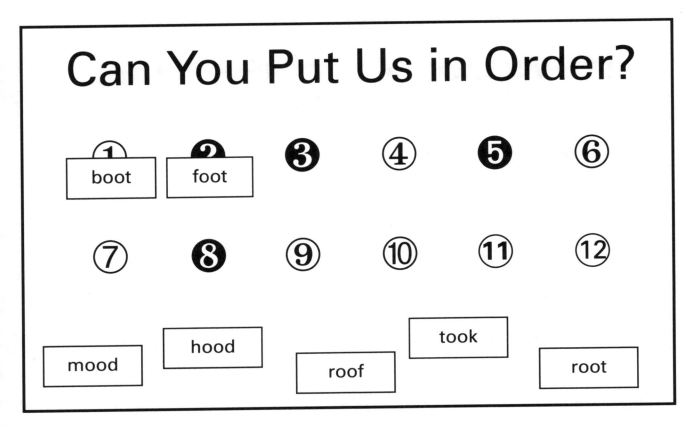

How Do You Spell That?

OBJECTIVE

Children will practice word recognition and matching shapes.

DIRECTIONS

1. Place title on board.
2. Cut construction-paper rectangles in half, like puzzle pieces.
3. Place an object from a magazine picture on one half of the rectangle and the spelling for that word on the matching half.
4. For older students, include several common misspellings of the words on matching pieces.
5. Place all the picture pieces in one envelope and the word pieces in another. Ask children to match pictures and correct spellings and to pin puzzle pieces to board.

How Do You Spell That?

PICTURES

WORDS

What's in a Sentence?

OBJECTIVE

Children will practice noun/verb, adjective/adverb recognition; capitalization; and punctuation while creating sentences.

DIRECTIONS

1. Arrange title on board. Stick rows of pins an equal distance apart across board as shown.
2. Give each child two pieces of 4" × 8" card stock. Make extra cards for articles—"a," "the," etc.—and other words that might be needed. Punch a hole at the top of each card.
3. Ask some children to think of two-word sentences—dogs run—and write them, one word on each card. Leave out capitalization and punctuation. Ask other children to write two adjectives or two adverbs. Place cards in an envelope near the bulletin board.
4. Place small circles with abbreviations for "noun, verb, adjective, adverb, capital letter" in an envelope near the board. Include small circles with end-of-sentence punctuation marks—period, question mark, exclamation point.
5. Children build sentences by hanging word cards on pins, then pin the appropriate circle above each word.

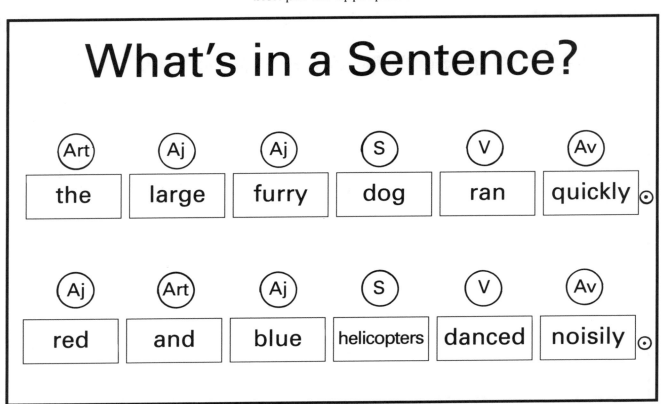

How Far Did Your Lunch Travel?

OBJECTIVE

Children will learn that the foods we eat are grown and produced in different areas of our country. Children will thank God for His abundant gifts.

DIRECTIONS

1. Place title and a large United States (or Canadian) map on the board.

2. Ask children to bring food labels from home or to save them from items in their school lunchroom.

3. Help children use social science texts, library books, and encyclopedias to identify locations where the main ingredient in each food item is grown or produced.

4. On the map, help children pin yarn from the location where the food is produced out to the sides of the map, where they may pin the yarn to their labels.

5. Place a small picture of your school in the appropriate spot on the map. Help children measure the distance from your school to the place where each item is produced.

6. Using your map's legend, help children calculate the approximate distance that each food "traveled." Display that number of miles/kilometers on a card next to each label.

7. Encourage children to thank God for the variety of foods He gives us and for the many people who help grow and produce it.

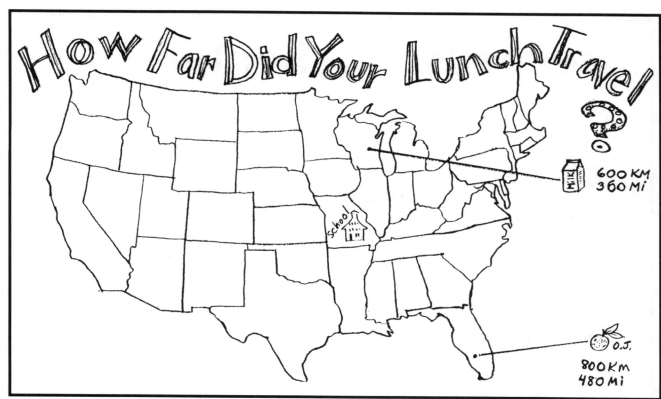

Can You Solve the Great Color Mix-up?

OBJECTIVE

Children will learn about "mixing" colors to create new colors.

DIRECTIONS

1. Divide bulletin board into four sections covered with gray, green, orange, and purple construction paper. Label each section with appropriate color name. Stick two pins in each section. Attach title to the top of the board.
2. Let children practice mixing colors of tempera paint to create new colors—blue and red make purple, etc.
3. Cut the following shapes from construction paper: White and black triangles, blue and yellow circles, red and yellow squares, and blue and red rectangles. Punch a hole at the top of each shape.
4. Let children review "mixing" colors by hanging appropriate shapes on each background.

Can You Solve the Great Color Mix-up?

Gray	Green	Orange	Purple

What Have Your Senses Told You Today?

OBJECTIVE

Children will thank God for giving them their senses to explore His world and record times when they use their senses to experience His blessings.

DIRECTIONS

1. Divide board into five sections labeled *Smell, Taste, Sight, Hearing, Touch.* Place title across top of board.
2. Cut paper rectangles and store them in an envelope or box near board.
3. Explain to children that God gave us our five senses so that we can explore and enjoy the world He made for us. Show children how to write sentences about what they experience through their senses. Have children pin their sentences to the appropriate section on the board. For example, "This pizza tastes great!" would be pinned under *Taste.* "This hamster is really soft!" would be pinned under *Touch.* Children may illustrate their sentences if they wish.
4. Ask children to participate in a circle prayer, thanking God for giving them senses to explore His creation.

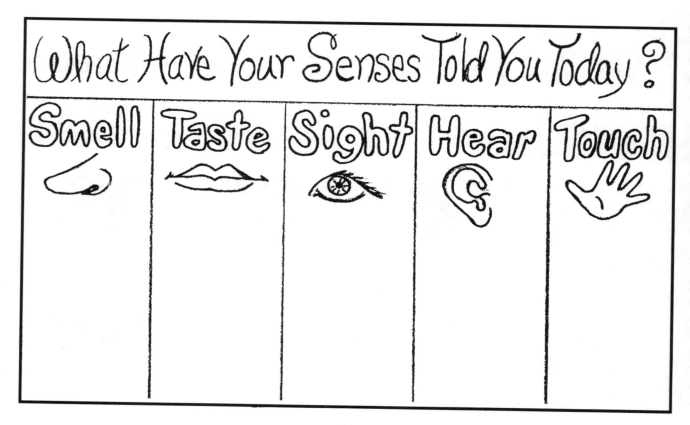

Who's Alive?

OBJECTIVE

Children will explore God's creation and categorize pictures of living and nonliving things.

DIRECTIONS

1. Place title and "Living" and "Nonliving" signs on bulletin board. Place pins on board so children can hang pictures.
2. Cut out magazine pictures of living and nonliving things and mount on index cards. Punch a hole at the top of each card.
3. Store cards in an envelope or box close to bulletin board. To play, children hang cards in the appropriate section. If you wish to make the game self-checking, write "Living" in one color and put matching dots on the back of each "living" picture. Use a different color for nonliving objects.

What Kind of Vertebrate Am I?

OBJECTIVE

Children will identify vertebrate animals and label them with appropriate animal group.

DIRECTIONS

1. Place title in the "sky" on board. Create an outdoor scene with trees, pond, grass, rocks, etc., cut from construction paper.
2. Have children cut out pictures (or draw) vertebrates and staple them to the scene in an area where they would live.
3. Make about 10 labels for the following groups: bird, fish, reptile, amphibian, and mammal. Hang the labels incorrectly on pins near each animal.
4. Ask children to arrange the labels correctly, then mix them up for the next player.

How Many Today, Mr. Phalange?

OBJECTIVE

Children will identify numbers grouped in tens.

DIRECTIONS

1. Use the pattern from the next page and cut construction paper to make a Mr. Phalange, as shown. Use string for arms, or simply draw arms on bulletin board background.

2. Ask children to trace both hands on a piece of paper. Show them how to cut out their tracing, leaving both hand prints on the cut paper.

3. Trace your own hand nine times, showing the digits from 1 to 9.

4. Each day choose a number—53, 87, etc.—and pin the appropriate hands to Mr. Phalange's arms so his fingers equal that number.

5. Children may take turns counting by tens and ones and writing the day's number on Mr. Phalange's tummy.

6. When children have mastered the game, you may wish to ask them to place hands on Mr. Phalange's arms and let another child count and write the correct number.

Pattern for Mr. Phalange

What Shape Are You In?

OBJECTIVE

Children will make and identify geometric shapes.

DIRECTIONS

1. Pin title and two large pieces of felt on board.
2. Cut sixteen 8" × 1" strip of various colors of felt. (Avoid background color.)
3. Pin a list of the geometric shapes you are teaching the children by each large felt piece.
4. Pin a marker—a construction-paper star will work—by each list.
5. To play, one child builds two shapes from felt strips and another child moves the markers to the correct name for each shape.

What Shape Are You In ?

square
rhombus
rectangle
pentagon ☆
hexagon

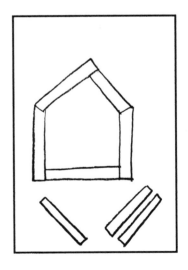
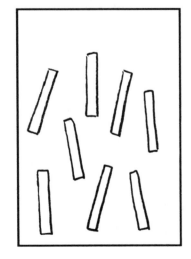

square
rhombus
rectangle
pentagon
hexagon

Choose Your Challenge!

OBJECTIVE

Children will practice multiplication facts.

DIRECTIONS

1. Pin letters for title and construction-paper rectangles reading " × 1, × 2 . . . × 10" to board. Stick an extra pin by each rectangle.

2. Number large sheets of construction paper with numerals 2–10. Punch two holes at the top of each sheet and connect them with ring fasteners. Push pins through the rings to hang sheets on bulletin board.

3. Cut out 42 circles, squares, or seasonal shapes. Number each with a product from the 1–10 multiplication table. Include all possible products: 1–10, 12, 14, 15, 16, 18, 20, 21, 24, 25, 27, 28, 30, 32, 35, 36, 40, 42, 45, 48, 49, 50, 54, 56, 60, 63, 64, 70, 72, 80, 81, 90, 100.

4. Group the shapes into envelopes labeled "ONES," "TENS," "TWENTIES," etc. Attach envelopes to board.

5. To play, children flip the large number sheets to the factor of their choice. As quickly as possible they search through the envelopes and hang up the correct answer. For example, if the factor 4 is chosen on the large sheet, they must hang the small shape 8 on the "× 2" pin.

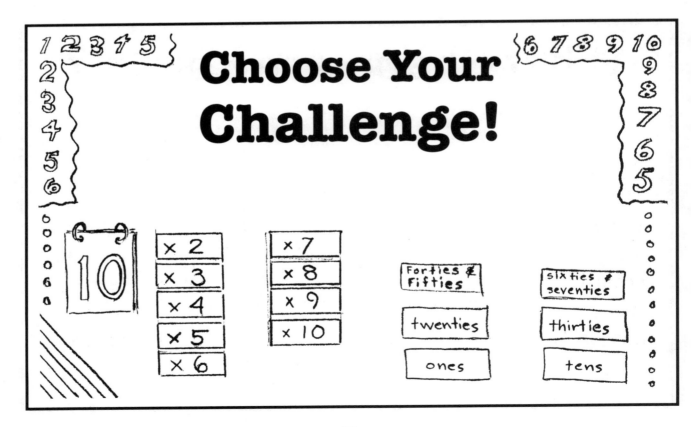

How Did God Use . . . ?

OBJECTIVE

Children will identify facts about Bible characters they are studying and how God used them to accomplish His will.

DIRECTIONS

1. Place title on board.
2. Divide board into sections labeled with the name of each biblical character being studied.
3. Divide children into small groups. Each group should write three facts about their character, or the way God used that character to carry out His purpose, on index cards.
4. Punch holes at tops of cards and hang them in mixed-up order. Children must hang the correct facts in each character's section.

How Is God Using . . . ?

OBJECTIVE

Children will encourage one another as they see evidence of God's Holy Spirit working in the lives of their classmates.

DIRECTIONS

1. Place title on board.
2. Ask children to decorate envelopes with their names. Attach envelopes to board.
3. Place small squares of paper in an envelope or box nearby.
4. When children see a classmate sharing God's love, they may write a simple sentence on a square of paper, describing what they saw, and place the square in that child's envelope. (You may want to use this bulletin board in conjunction with "How Did God Use . . . ?")

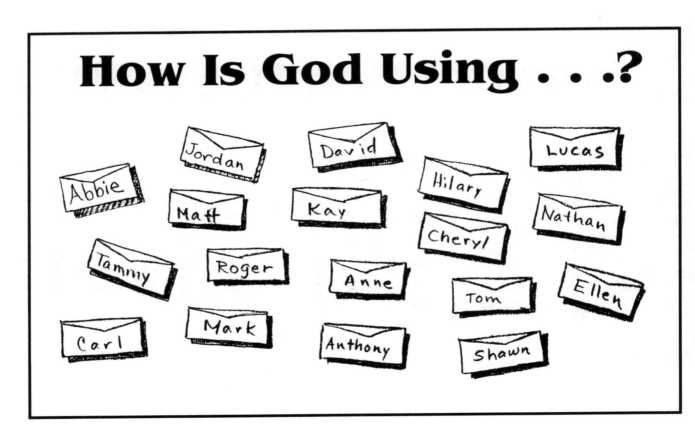

What Gifts Can You Use?

OBJECTIVE

The children will learn to use and thank God for His gifts recorded in Rom. 12:6–8.

DIRECTIONS

1. Place title on board.
2. Enlarge the pattern on the next page. Mark each puzzle piece with one of the gifts recorded in Romans 12: prophesying, serving, teaching, encouraging, giving, leading, showing mercy.
3. Add one puzzle piece to the board a day, explaining the gift and how God's children can serve Him and each other with that gift.
4. When the puzzle is complete, you may wish to duplicate the pattern on the next page and ask children to write down the names of children and school/church staff in the puzzle pieces which they feel match their gifts.

(Fill in words of your choice)

Pattern for "Learn to Use Them" Puzzle

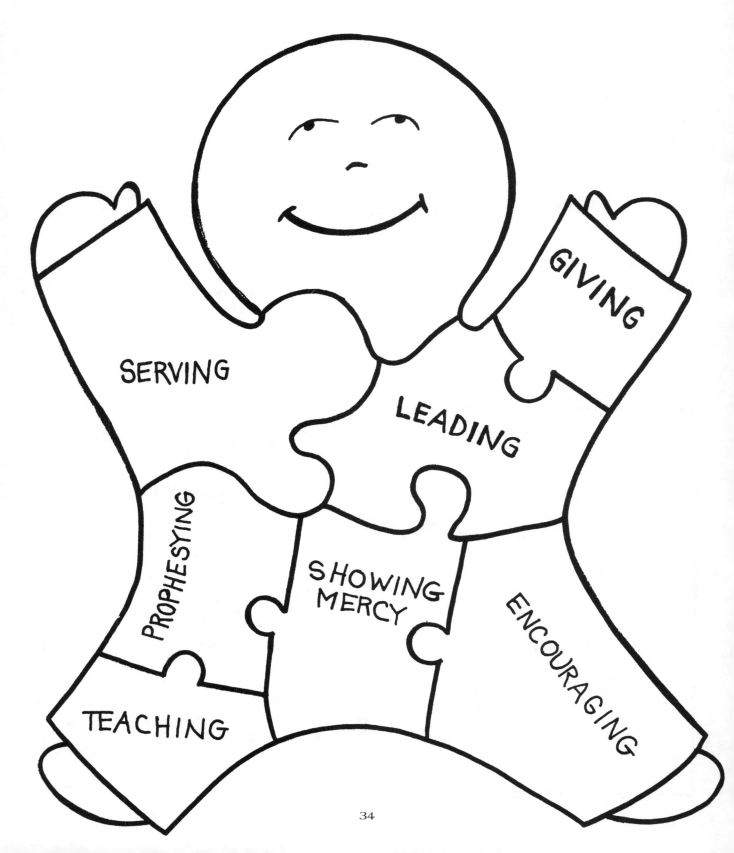

How Do You Describe the Rock?

OBJECTIVE

Children will learn the meaning of Bible verses that describe God as a rock.

DIRECTIONS

1. Place letters for title and rocks cut from construction paper on board.
2. Write the following scrambled words describing God as our rock on strips of paper: *Perfect* (Deut. 32:4); *Deliverer* (2 Sam. 22:2); *Refuge* (2 Sam. 22:3); *Fortress* (Ps. 18:2); *Redeemer* (Ps. 19:14); *Eternal* (Is. 26:4); *Precious* (Is. 28:16b); *Sure* (Is. 28:16b).
3. Each day attach one scrambled word on the board. Give children time to unscramble the letters.
4. At the close of the day, read the corresponding Bible verse and explain how the words describing God as a rock assure us of His love and care. Write the word correctly on a slip of paper and ask a child to pin it over the scrambled words.

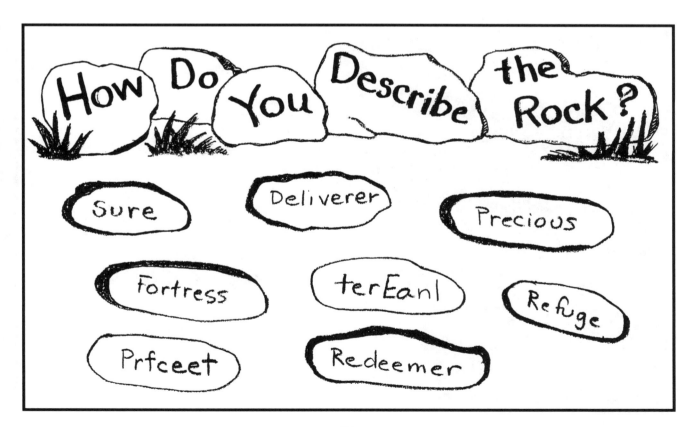

Nothing but the Blood of Jesus

OBJECTIVE

The children will create a reminder that only the blood of Jesus can wash away our sin.

DIRECTIONS

1. Hang crumpled, ripped, smudged background paper on one half of the board.
2. Hang smooth, clean paper on the other half of the board.
3. Cut letters for the title from red construction paper and place on clean side of the board. (You may wish to write the letters with red chalk or marker.)
4. Cut a large cross from construction paper and place it in the middle of the board.
5. Ask children to draw a picture of a sin they have committed. Then have them crumple and tear their sins and pin them to the crumpled half of the board.
6. Pray together. Thank God for sending His Son to die on the cross to pay the price for our sins and win us forgiveness.

What Comes Next?

OBJECTIVE

Children will learn to place the seasons of the church year in order and identify a symbol with each season that helps them remember God's plan for their salvation.

DIRECTIONS

1. Place title on the board.
2. Write cards with corresponding construction-paper symbols for the following church seasons/festivals: Advent, Advent wreath; Christmas, manger; Epiphany, star; Transfiguration, mountain and cloud; Lent, cross; Easter, butterfly; Ascension, clouds in blue circle; Pentecost, tongue of fire; Trinity, 3 intersecting circles; Reformation, Luther's coat of arms; All Saints' Day, shield.
3. As you study the different seasons of the church year, ask a child to pin the name of the season to the board with its corresponding symbol. Children may mix up the seasons and symbols and place them in correct order. Draw a key for the correct order/symbols and keep it in a folder near the board, so children can check their work.

Will You Pray for Me?

OBJECTIVE

Children will learn to use a Bible concordance as they comfort one another with the promises God makes to us in His Word.

DIRECTIONS

1. Make a name tag for each child. Place title and name tags on board. Place a Bible concordance close to the board.
2. Make one stack of gray rain clouds and one stack of white clouds.
3. When children have a prayer request, ask them to write it on a rain cloud and pin it face down under their name tag.
4. Classmates may use the concordance to find a Bible verse about God's love, healing, or care. They may write the verse on a white cloud and pin it over the rain cloud of the child who made the request.
5. Take time each day to pray for the children who have made requests. If children are too young to use a concordance, you can help them write God's promises on white clouds so they are ready to use when prayers are requested.

Go Fish!

OBJECTIVE

Children will understand Jesus' command to be fishers of men and share their faith in Jesus with others.

DIRECTIONS

1. Place title on a blue background. Attach a construction-paper fishing pole with yarn for the line. Tie the end of the yarn (where the hook would be) around a construction paper cross.
2. Place several fish patterns and appropriate colors of construction paper close to the board.
3. Share your faith with the children and roleplay situations where the children share their faith with family members and friends.
4. When children talk to someone about Christ, they may write that person's name on a fish and attach it to board. You may want to include names of people to whom children want to witness so the class can pray for them.

On Christ the Solid Rock I Stand

OBJECTIVE

Children will create a display with the understanding that Christ is the solid Rock upon whom their faith is based.

DIRECTIONS

1. Place title on board.
2. Cut a large sheet of construction paper or brown wrapping paper in the shape of a rock. Crumple paper and attach to board.
3. Add construction paper waves and sun.
4. Ask each child to use markers, crayons, or cut paper to make their two legs.
5. Attach legs to bulletin board so feet are standing on the rock. Add clouds to cover the tops of legs.

Waiting for Jesus . . . What Did They Do?

OBJECTIVE

Students will learn that God used His people, even though they were sinners, to accomplish His will as they waited for the Messiah to be born.

DIRECTIONS

1. Place title on bulletin board.
2. Write the name of Old Testament characters who waited for the Messiah on construction paper stars.
3. As you study each character, write some of that person's sins or shortcomings on a small piece of paper. Smudge and crumple the paper and attach it to the character's star to remind the class that this character dealt with the same problem we do—sin.
4. As you study how God used His people and forgave their sins, place brightly colored stars over the crumpled paper.

Give Them All to Jesus

OBJECTIVE

Children will understand that God will help them bear their worries and burdens when they give them to Him in prayer (1 Peter 5:7).

DIRECTIONS

1. Place title on board.
2. Ask each child to write a burden or worry on a 4" × 6" card.
3. Put out gift wrap, ribbon, scissors, and tape. Ask children to gift wrap their worries.
4. Place gifts on board.

Help Us Shine

OBJECTIVE

Children will use star shapes to develop visual discrimination and eye/hand coordination.

DIRECTIONS

1. Place letters of title on board.
2. Cut out 10–15 stars in various shapes and sizes.
3. Trace star shapes on background paper of bulletin board.
4. Pin stars at bottom of board. To play, children pin stars in their correct spaces.

Will You Share God's Gift?

OBJECTIVE

Children will remember the gifts God gives to them and share them with others.

DIRECTIONS

1. Place title on bulletin board.
2. Make a construction paper fireplace and attach it to board.
3. Ask each child to cut two matching construction paper stockings. Staple, glue, or tape sides together, leaving top open. Children should write their names on their stockings, decorate them, and hang them on the fireplace.
4. Every few days, put a paper heart, cross, or other specially shaped note with a simple message in the children's stockings. A heart might say, "Jesus loves you." A cross might say, "God sent His own Son to die for you." (Paper-clipping the shape to the inside of the stocking works well.)
5. Talk about the meaning of the message and encourage the children to give the note to a family member or friend who needs to know about Jesus' love.

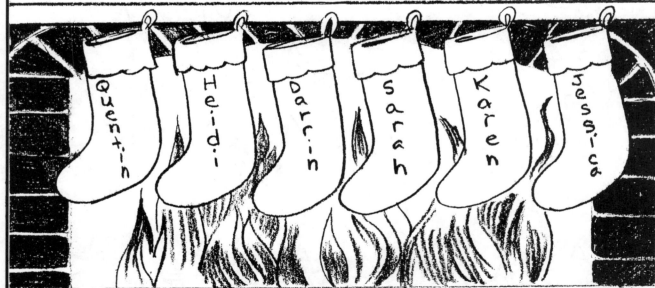

And It Came to Pass . . .

OBJECTIVE

Children will practice measuring skills as they make figures for a crèche scene.

DIRECTIONS

1. Place title on board.
2. Approximate sizes of crèche figures. Suggested measurements for a large board: Mary, 15"; Joseph, 17"; Baby Jesus in manger, 5"; Shepherds, 13–17"; Angels, 15"; sheep, 5–6" long; cow, 11" long; donkey, 9" long; trees, 21–25"; star, 7 .
3. Give each child materials—markers, crayons, paints, etc.— to make their figures the assigned size. Display crèche figures on board.

How Deep Is the Snow at Your House?

OBJECTIVE

Children will decorate houses to place on hills of snow and practice measuring skills.

DIRECTIONS

1. Arrange title, sky, and snow scene on bulletin board. Help children make and decorate paper houses and write their initials on them.
2. Pin houses along the hills and valleys of snow.
3. Ask children to measure the depth of the snow from the bottom of their house to the bottom of the board. Continue moving houses until the children have measured all the hills and valleys. (You may wish to cut a new snow scene and have the children measure again, or measure again using a different unit of measurement.)

How Deep Is the Snow at Your House?

Melt the Snowman!

OBJECTIVE

Children will use a snowman game to practice subtraction facts with a partner.

DIRECTIONS

1. Place title and "snowy" border on board.
2. Cut out 43 white circles (4" in diameter).

3. Add faces and hats to three of the circles. Divide the other 40 circles into two groups, numbering each group from 1 to 20. Punch a hole at the top of each of these 40 circles.
4. Attach the snowmen's heads to the board as shown. Stick four straight pins in a vertical row below each head so that children can hang numbers on them. Place a half circle of snow marked with a 0 (zero) underneath each head at the bottom of the board.
5. Store the numbered circles near the board in groups of 1–20, and 11–20, so the children can sort through them easily.
6. Help children play as partners. The first partner places numbers on the pins, with the numbers getting smaller top to bottom. The other child states what must be subtracted from each number to get to the next number, until the snowman is melted to zero.

Can You Dress Us?

OBJECTIVE

Children will match patterns they create on hats and boots.

DIRECTIONS

1. Arrange title, snowmen, and snow scene on board.
2. Have each child make matching boots and hats for the snowmen. Punch a hole at the top of each boot and hat and store them close to the board.
3. Place one pin at the top and two pins at the bottom of each snowman, where children may hang hat and boots.
4. Let children take turns hanging matching hat and boots on each snowman.

Can You Give Squeaky a Boost?

OBJECTIVE

Children will understand that the love God shares with us shows us how to love one another, and they will work together to achieve a goal.

DIRECTIONS

1. Arrange title, a snowy hill, and a small snowball on board. Add snowflakes made by the children.
2. Copy pattern for "Squeaky" and trace and color with markers, or reproduce on gray or black construction paper.
3. Make several consecutively larger snowballs.
4. Explain to the children that the love God shares with us through Jesus helps us to love one another. Pray with the children. Ask God's help with a specific response to His love, such as forgiving one another. Exchange the snowball for a larger one, helping Squeaky "push" the snowball up the hill, each time the children exhibit this behavior.

Pattern for "Can You Give Squeaky a Boost?"

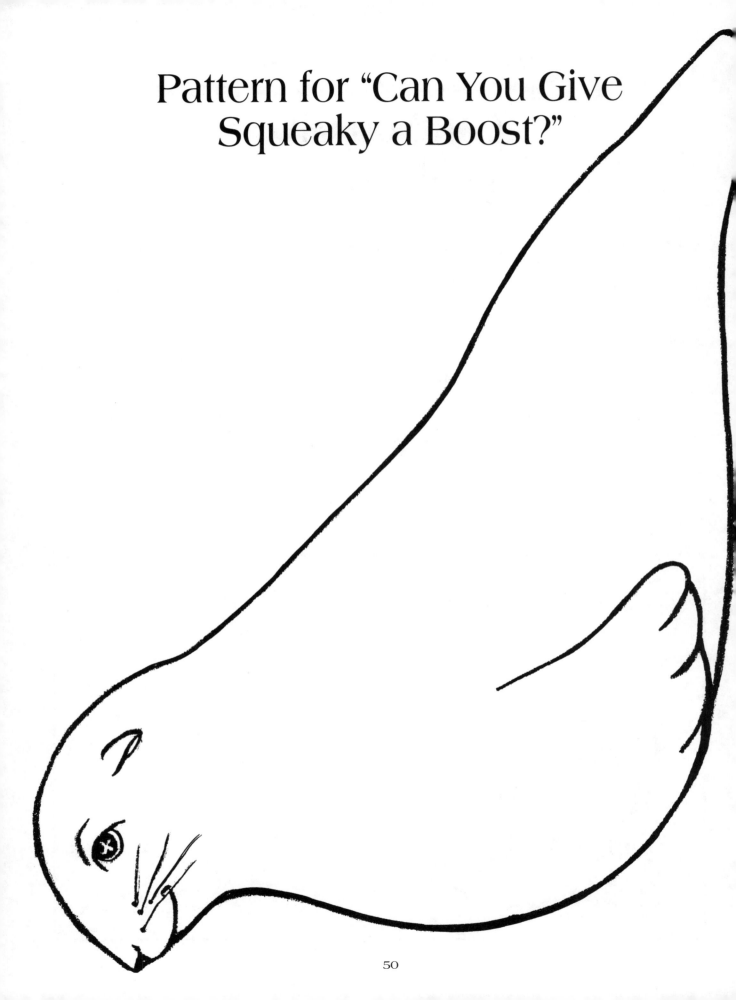

It's Cool to Be in Jesus' Flock

OBJECTIVE

Children will sponge-paint snowflakes and create penguins as they celebrate the fellowship we share in Jesus.

DIRECTIONS

1. Attach title to board. Help children sponge-paint snowflakes on board background. (Children may also cut paper snowflakes.)
2. Copy and enlarge the penguin on the next page to make several tagboard patterns.
3. Help each child create a penguin, using crayons, markers, or colored construction paper. (Displaying several pictures of penguins will be helpful.)
4. Hang penguins on bulletin board. Thank God for the joyful fellowship we share as His children.

Pattern for "It's Cool to Be in Jesus' Flock"

You Covered All Our Sins

OBJECTIVE

Children will confess their sins and rejoice in the forgiveness God grants us through the life, death, and resurrection of His Son.

DIRECTIONS

1. Cover board with a medium blue paper background. Draw the outline of a hill at the bottom of the board and add title.
2. Encourage the children to anonymously write some recent sins on the hill in quiet moments, and ask God to forgive them. (Write your sins as well!)
3. Pray together. Thank God for sending His Son to pay the price for our sins.
4. Help the children take turns painting white paint over their sins and adding cut paper or painted snowflakes. (In February you may wish to add red hearts with children's names.)

How Can We Share God's Love?

OBJECTIVE

Children will decorate hearts to create a bulletin board and carry out creative actions to share God's love.

DIRECTIONS

1. Place title on board.
2. Ask each child to decorate a heart. Pin hearts to board.
3. Under each heart write a special activity that children can do as a class or individually to share God's love: Sing a song about Jesus for the principal. Make a "God is with you" card for a teacher or child who is sick. Share crayons with your partner, etc.

"My Words Will Never Pass Away"

OBJECTIVE

Children will write a favorite promise of God and understand that God's promises last forever.

DIRECTIONS

1. Attach letters of Mark 13:31 and melting snowmen to board.
2. Ask each child to fold a piece of paper in half. Decorate the front page as a Bible and write a favorite promise of God inside.
3. Display Bibles on bulletin board. Discuss one promise each day and thank God for keeping that promise.

Help Us Bloom Quickly!

OBJECTIVE

Children will increase speed and accuracy in learning addition facts.

DIRECTIONS

1. Place letters of title and groupings of flower stems (painted or cut from green construction paper) on board. Label each stem grouping with a sum, 10–15. Place straight pins at spots where flowers will hang.
2. Cut 36 flowers from a variety of colored construction paper. Label each flower with an addend combination. (See key on next page.) Punch hole at the top of each flower.
3. Copy and distribute a time/trial sheet and answer key for each child.
4. To play, children time one another in putting the flowers on correct stems and check their work against the key.

Answer Key and Time/Trial Sheet
for "Help Us Bloom Quickly"

ANSWER KEY

10: 1+9, 2+8, 3+7, 4+6, 5+5
11: 1+10, 2+9, 3+8, 4+7, 5+6
12: 1+11, 2+10, 3+9, 4+6, 5+7, 6+6
13: 1+12, 2+11, 3+10, 4+9, 5+8, 6+7
14: 1+13, 2+12, 3+11, 4+10, 5+9, 6+8, 7+7
15: 1+14, 2+13, 3+12, 4+11, 5+10, 6+9, 7+8

Help Us Bloom Quickly!

Name _____

Trial	Time	# Correct
_____	_____	_____
_____	_____	_____
_____	_____	_____
_____	_____	_____
_____	_____	_____

Good Job! Keep Improving!

What's New?

OBJECTIVE

Children will add objects to a spring bulletin board, thanking God for new growth and the new life Jesus brings.

DIRECTIONS

1. Arrange letters of title and a bare winter landscape on board.
2. Help children look for signs of spring: Leaves budding on trees, grass turning green, flowers blooming, baby animals, etc. Remind children that because God raised Jesus from the dead on Easter morning, we all enjoy a new life with Jesus now and will live forever with Him in heaven one day.
3. Children may add leaves to trees, grass, flowers, pictures of baby animals cut from magazines, etc.

God's Spirit Helps Us Grow

OBJECTIVE

Children will help make a bulletin board and ask God's help in living Christ-like lives.

DIRECTIONS

1. Arrange title and seed packets on board. Label packets with Christ-like qualities you will encourage in the children.
2. Give groups of children vegetable patterns and have them trace and cut enough vegetables to fill each row. Collect vegetables.
3. Explain that God's Holy Spirit comes to us in our Baptism and through God's Word to help us grow in faith. Talk about how Jesus exhibited each quality during His life on earth. Pray for God's help in living out these qualities.
4. When you see a child exhibiting one of these qualities, give him/her a vegetable to staple to the correct row.

Who Will Gather the Eggs?

OBJECTIVE

Children will practice visual discrimination as they sort Easter eggs.

DIRECTIONS

1. Place title and 4 or 5 construction-paper Easter baskets on board.
2. Ask each child to design two Easter eggs, decorating them with markers, crayons, paint, or cut paper.
3. Pin the eggs across the bottom of the board.
4. Children may sort eggs by color, design, or any other characteristic and pin them in appropriate basket.

The Cross, Crafted by You, Carried by Him

OBJECTIVE

Children will confess their sins on a cross puzzle and thank Jesus for paying the price for their sins and winning them forgiveness.

DIRECTIONS

1. Arrange title on board. Cut out two, large identical crosses.
2. Cut one cross into enough puzzle pieces so that each child may have a piece.
3. Ask each child to anonymously write a recent sin on a puzzle piece. Assemble the puzzle, stapling pieces to the board. (For younger children, draw the puzzle pieces and leave cross assembled on board. Let children take turns writing a simple sentence or drawing a picture of their sins on the pieces.)
4. Encourage children to pray silently and confess their sins to God.
5. Cover puzzle cross with a complete cross. Explain that Jesus died to take the punishment for our sins and that God gives us complete forgiveness.

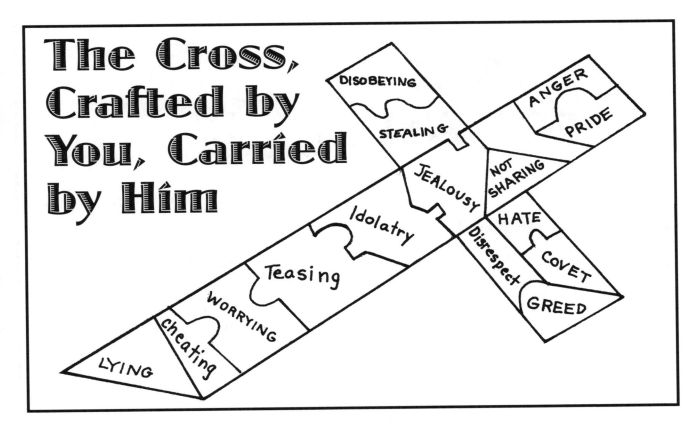

Once for All

OBJECTIVE

Children will confess their sins by writing them on slips of paper and understand that Jesus died to suffer the punishment for our sins.

DIRECTIONS

1. Place title and large cross with the words of Is. 53:5 on board.
2. Keep a supply of small squares of paper by board. Allow children to quietly write down a sin, confess their sin to God, and fold the paper in half and staple to cross.
3. Help children remember that Jesus suffered the punishment for our sins when He died on the cross.

ONCE FOR ALL

Hebrews 10:10

Jesus:

He was pierced for our transgressions, He was crushed for our iniquities; the punishment that brought us peace was upon Him. Isaiah 53:5

God Made You a Winner . . . Tell Somebody!

OBJECTIVE

Children will rejoice in the new life and forgiveness Jesus won for them, and share that good news with others.

DIRECTIONS

1. Place title on board. Trace cross used for "Once for All" to make a new cross.
2. Write or paint words of 1 Corinthians 15:57 on cross: "Thanks be to God! He gives us the victory through our Lord Jesus Christ."
3. Make construction-paper flowers and butterflies. Write a phrase such as "He Is Risen!" or "Jesus Won the Victory" on each one. (You may wish to ask children to make objects before Easter, but don't explain what they are for!)
4. Pin the flowers and butterflies on the cross until the verse is covered.
5. Let children uncover the cross, one object at a time, and decide with whom they will share the good news that Jesus is alive.

Free to Serve

OBJECTIVE

Children will create a display celebrating their freedom in Christ.

DIRECTIONS

1. If desired, help children dip their palms in a shallow dish of tempera paint and print hand prints as a background for the board.
2. Place title on board.
3. Show children how to trace two hand prints side-by-side to create a butterfly wing. Assemble butterflies on board with four hand prints extending from the body of the butterfly to form the wings.
4. Add chenille craft sticks for antennae and pin to board.
5. Explain to children that the butterfly is a resurrection symbol. The butterfly breaks free from its cocoon to enjoy new life. The new life Jesus won for us on the cross frees us from sin, death, and the devil so that we may serve Him.